FastTrack
MUSIC INSTRUCTION

E-flat
Saxophone 1

T0033996

INTRODUCTION

You bought a saxophone...so now what?

Congratulations! You look great holding that new saxophone (even standing in front of the mirror, air-playing to the radio). But won't your friends and family be even more impressed if you can actually play the darn thing?

In just a few weeks, we'll have you playing some very well-known tunes, as well as jamming with some cool riffs and techniques. By the end of this book, you'll be ready to play with a band and play the hits—The Beatles, Clapton, Hendrix, and more.

All we ask is that you observe the three Ps: **patience, practice,** and **pace yourself.**

Don't try to bite off more than you can chew, and DON'T skip ahead. If your lips hurt, take the day off. If you get frustrated, put it down and come back later. If you forget something, go back and learn it again. If you're having a great time, forget about dinner and keep on playing. Most importantly, have fun!

ABOUT THE AUDIO

We're glad you noticed the added bonus—audio tracks! Each music example in the book is included, so you can hear how it sounds and play along when you're ready. Take a listen whenever you see this symbol: ◆❶

Each audio example is preceded by one measure of "clicks" to indicate the tempo and meter. Pan right to hear the sax part emphasized. Pan left to hear the accompaniment emphasized. As you become more confident, try playing along with the rest of the band.

To access audio visit:
www.halleonard.com/mylibrary

Enter Code
2807-5204-2345-1662

ISBN 978-0-7935-8713-1

Saxophone featured on front cover provided courtesy of Cascio Music.

HAL•LEONARD®
CORPORATION
7777 W. BLUEMOUND RD. P.O. BOX 13819 MILWAUKEE, WI 53213

Visit Hal Leonard online at
www.halleonard.com

A GOOD PLACE TO START

Your sax is your friend

An instrument can be like a good friend over the years—get you through the rough times and help you sing away the blues. So, before we get started, let's give your sax a name.

What a beauty!

Below are pictures of the various parts of an alto saxophone. Get acquainted with these parts, and (most importantly) learn the proper way to put them together (explained on the next page)…

Reed

Mouthpiece Cover

Mouthpiece

Body

Ligature

Neck No Mouth

Neck Strap

REED ME: Reeds are numbered. The higher the number, the more difficult to get a good sound. So, start with a "2" or "2 1/2" and work your way up as you become more advanced.

PUTTING IT ALL TOGETHER

A bit confused? Here's a play-by-play of "building" your saxophone:

 Find the **neckstrap** and put it around your neck (duh!).

 Slide the **mouthpiece** gently onto the cork end of the **neck**. Try twisting it slightly as you push. If you hear a squeak, or if it feels too tight, apply some cork grease to the cork and try again. (You can find cork grease at most musical instrument stores.) The mouthpiece should cover about three-fourths of the cork (not the entire cork).

Mouth without reed

 Put the thin part of the **reed** in your mouth for about 30 seconds to moisten it. (NOTE: You can do steps 2 and 3 at the same time.)

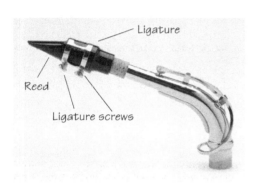

Ligature

Reed

Ligature screws

 Place the reed on the **mouthpiece**. The flat side of the reed goes against the flat part of the mouth-piece (makes sense, huh?).

 Slide the **ligature** into place (over the reed and mouthpiece) while holding the reed with your thumb. The reed should be positioned so that only a hairline of black mouthpiece is visible behind the reed.

 Tighten the **ligature screws** firmly (but not too firmly).

 Insert the **neck** (with mouthpiece) into the **body** of the sax. (Make sure to loosen the screw at the top of the body first!)

 Hook the **neckstrap** onto the **body** of the sax and make any necessary adjustments to the strap for a comfortable hold. The mouthpiece should be level with your mouth when you're standing.

Sax with strap

DOG-EAR THESE TWO PAGES
(...you'll need to review them later)

Music is a language with its own symbols, structure, rules (and exceptions to those rules). To read, write, and play music requires knowing all the symbols and rules. But let's take it one step at a time (a few now, a few later)...

Notes

Music is written with little doo-hickeys called **notes.** Notes come in all shapes and sizes. A note has two essential characteristics: its **pitch** (indicated by its position on the staff) and its **rhythmic value** (indicated by the following symbols):

| whole note | half note | quarter note |

The rhythmic value lets you know how many beats the note lasts. Most commonly, a quarter note equals one beat. After that it's just like fractions (we hate math, too!):

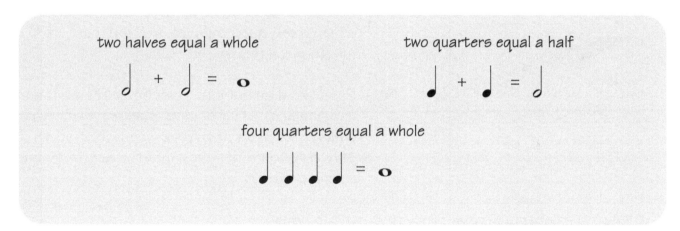

two halves equal a whole

two quarters equal a half

four quarters equal a whole

Staff

All the notes are positioned on (or nearby) a **staff,** which consists of five parallel lines and four spaces. (The plural for staff is "staves.") Each line and space represent a different pitch.

Leger Lines

Since not all notes will fit on just five lines and four spaces, **leger lines** (pronounced like "ledger") are used to extend the staff:

Clef

A symbol called a **clef** indicates which pitches appear on a particular staff. Music uses a variety of clefs, but we are only concerned with one:

Treble clef

A **treble clef** staff makes the lines and spaces have the following pitches:

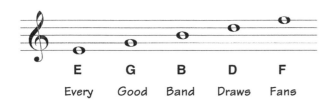

E G B D F
Every Good Band Draws Fans

F A C E
"FACE"

An easy way to remember the line pitches is "Every Good Band Draws Fans." For the spaces, spell "**face**."

Measures (or Bars)

Notes on a staff are divided into **measures** (or "bars") to help you keep track of where you are in the song. (Imagine reading a book without any periods, commas, or capital letters!)

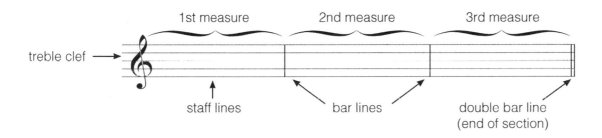

Time Signatures (or Meters)

A **time signature** (or "meter") indicates how many beats will appear in each measure. It contains two numbers: the top number tells you how many beats will be in each measure; the bottom number says what type of note will equal one beat.

four beats per measure
quarter note (1/4) = one beat

three beats per measure
quarter note (1/4) = one beat

Relax for a while, read through it again later, and then move on.
(Trust us — as we go through the book, you'll start to understand it.)

A FEW MORE THINGS

(before we begin)

Fingering diagrams picture a portion of your instrument's keys and show you where to place your fingers to play each note. Left-hand fingered keys are on top; right-hand fingered keys are on bottom.

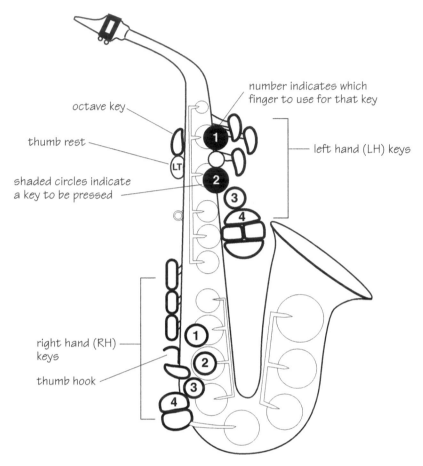

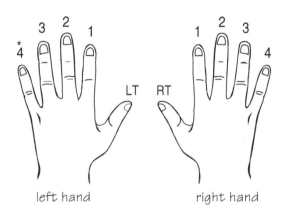

Think of your fingers as being numbered 1 through 4 (you can even mark them with a pen or fingernail polish, if you like.)

* Sad but true: we won't even use LH finger 4 in this book, but please don't cut it off...yet!

All thumbs?

Your left thumb should rest on the thumb rest (aptly named) just under the octave key, and your right thumb rests securely under the thumb hook (also aptly named).

LESSON 1
Don't just sit there, play something!

Now that you've assembled your sax and know how to hold it properly, let's make some music...

To play the sax requires a two-step process: select the note to be played by pressing appropriate keys with your fingers while blowing air through the mouthpiece of the sax. Sound easy? Give it a try.

Note : B

Press the top key (shown in the diagram below) with LH finger 1 and blow air through the sax until you hear your first note.

> PLAYING TIP: Your upper lip and top teeth should rest on the mouthpiece about three-eighths of an inch from the end. Your lower lip should press gently against the reed (but don't bite!).

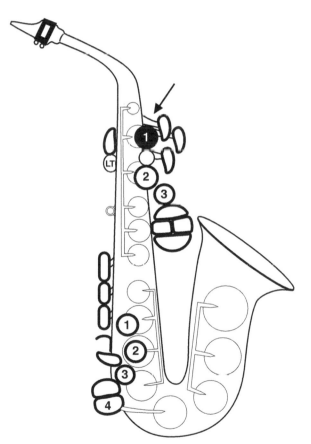

B lies on the middle line of the staff (flip back to page 5 for an easy way to remember the staff line names):

B

Congratulations! (Okay, sure, it squeaked and sounded awful, but that was your first try!) Relax and try again until you're pleased with the sound of the note.

Tonguing

Most of the time you'll want a definite beginning and end to each note. Such definition is accomplished by **tonguing**. Here's how...

 Say "ta" four times slowly. Notice where your tongue touches the roof of your mouth.

 Now say "ta" but hold it— "taaaaaaaaaaaaaaaaaa."

 Say it loud; whisper it.

That's how you "tongue" a note while playing the sax. By using the "ta" sound, you create a bit of an attack on the note that gives it a definite beginning. Easy enough?

Enough of that, let's jam!

Put the mouthpiece in your mouth and finger the note B. When you start to blow, tongue the note with a "ta." (If you need a quick review of rhythmic values or time signatures, flip back to page 4.):

◆❶ **Ta-Da!**

WHAT'S THAT? The " ❜ " symbol indicates an appropriate spot in the music to breathe (yeah, we think it's important, too!). Take a quick but deep breath whenever you see this symbol.

◆❷ **You B Jammin'**

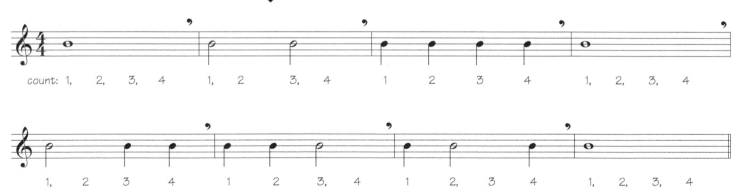

You can experiment with other tonguing sounds like "too" and "doo." Just for fun, try a fast tonguing with "ta-da, ta-da, ta-da" as you continue to blow steadily. Feel free to experiment (hey, it's your sax!).

TUNING TO THE AUDIO TRACK

An added feature of the **FastTrack**™ method is that you can play along with the audio. But unless your sax is in tune with the audio, you'll find it an unpleasant and frustrating experience. Don't panic—tuning is easy...

When you tune, you correct the pitch of your instrument. **Pitch** means how high or low a musical tone is. This is adjusted by tightening (or loosening) the mouthpiece on the cork.

Play the note B along with track 3. Your note will sound one of three ways:

1. **In tune**—Your note sounds the same as the track. Congratulations! Skip 2 and 3 and let's move on.

2. **Flat**—Your note sounds lower than the B on the track. Push the mouthpiece in slightly to raise the pitch.

3. **Sharp**—Your note sounds higher than the track. Pull the mouthpiece out slightly to lower the pitch.

Don't over-compensate. Push or pull only a little bit each time and try the note again.

TUNING MADE EASY: If you get a **flat**, you'll have to **push** your car to town.

LESSON 2

It takes two to tango...

Just one note (no matter how well it's played) can hardly be called music, so how 'bout another note?

> FINGERING MADE EASY: Throughout the book, **FastTrack**™ gives you easy ways to memorize note fingerings. Please make it a point to read these helpful hints whenever you see this icon:

Note: A

Still fingering B (with finger 1), simply add finger 2 for your new note.

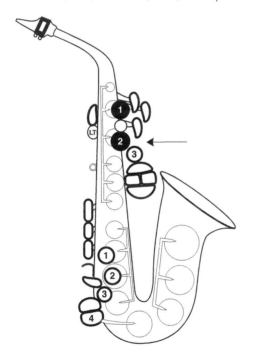

The note A lies on the space just below B (again, page 5 gives you an easy way to remember the space names):

A

 ADD A FINGER: As the notes go down from B, simply add a lower key. (What poetry?!)

Try your new note with your first note:

◆4 B 'n' A

SOME MORE NOTES ON MUSIC

(...pardon the pun!)

In addition to notes, you'll encounter other musical hieroglyphics as we go along...

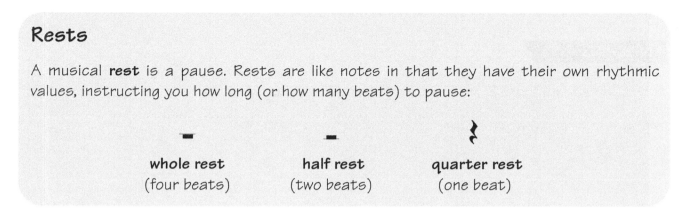

Rests

A musical **rest** is a pause. Rests are like notes in that they have their own rhythmic values, instructing you how long (or how many beats) to pause:

whole rest	half rest	quarter rest
(four beats)	(two beats)	(one beat)

Try it...

In the following 4/4 example, you will play A, A, pause, A, pause, pause, pause, pause, A, A, pause, pause, A, pause, pause, A:

◆5 Take a Load Off

IMPORTANT: a rest does not mean rest your fingers or put your sax down! During a rest you should take a quick breath and get your fingers into position for the next set of notes (okay, okay, but you'll learn more notes soon!):

◆6 Rock, Roll, Rest

Remember, just like reading a book, go on to the next line in the song until you see the double barline (the end).

LESSON 3

G, this is easy!

There are only so many tunes you can play with two notes and a few rests, so here's another note to make the music more interesting...

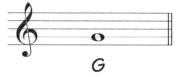

Note: G

For A, you added finger 2. Now just add finger 3 for your new note:

G lies (you guessed it!) on the line just below A. (The treble clef is sometimes called the "G-clef" since it circles around the G-line.)

G

 ADD A FINGER: One note lower than A requires adding one key lower than A.

Time for another work-out. Practice slowly and speed up the **tempo** only as you become more confident with the notes.

◆7 Three-Note Shuffle

YOU GOT RHYTHM

Nice tie!

A **tie** connects two notes (makes 'em look fancy) and tells you to extend the first note (keep playing) through to the end of the tied note:

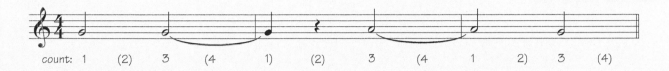

count: 1   (2)   3   (4)   1)   (2)   3   (4)   1   2)   3   (4)

Simple Simon! Remember to count the beat in your head as you play. Soon you'll begin to think and feel the beat as if it's second nature.

The ones with dots are nice, too!

Another way to extend the value of a note is to use a **dot**. A dot extends the note by one-half of its value. Most common is the **dotted half note**:

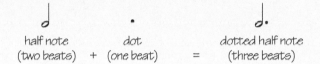

You'll encounter dotted half notes in many songs, especially those that use 3/4 meter (that is, three beats per measure) like track 8.

8 Three-Note Waltz

This is a good time to take a break, maybe order a pizza.
When you come back, wash the grease off your hands and review Lessons 1-3.

LESSON 4

Now let's C...

Three notes in three Lessons—great work! Let's go the other way this time with a higher note...

Note: C

Like B, your new note only requires one key to be pressed:

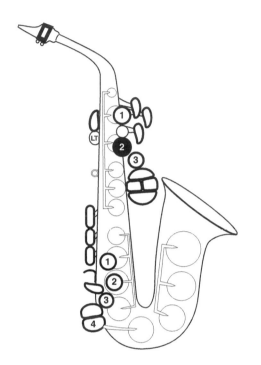

C lies on the space just above B (the first note you learned):

C

 FINGERING MADE EASY: From G to B, the informal rule is to lift a finger to play higher notes. Instead of a higher key than B, use a higher-numbered finger—finger 2.

Here comes a workout for your new note (along with a few of the old ones):

9 ◆ **Sax by the C**

Once you've got the hang of C, we can play some much better songs with all four of your notes:

10 C Me Rock

11 Barcarolle

12 Merrily We Rock 'n' Roll Along

LESSON 5
Don't forget the right hand!

S ince you've been so patient, we'll give you three new notes in this lesson (you're welcome!):

Notes: F, E, D

Let's get your right hand into the action (we told you on page 6 that poor ol' LH finger 4 would be skipped). Finger G with your left hand again and simply add the respective lower keys with the right hand:

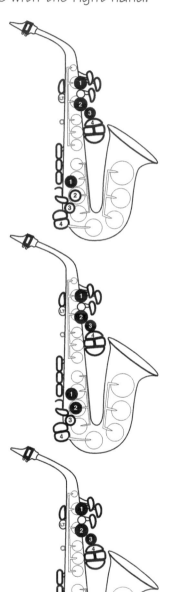

If it sounds lower than G, guess where it's written on the staff? Right—the space below:

One note lower is E, which lies on the first line of the staff:

D lies just below E (and just below the staff). We can still count this as a space, though:

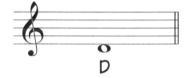

 ADD A FINGER: Start with your fingers on the G keys—as the notes go down, add right-hand keys going down.

The next (rather easy) exercise will get you acquainted with these three new notes:

⓭ D–E–F Jam

Seven notes for seven fingers...

Once you've learned F-E-D, play some more interesting songs with all seven of your notes:

⓮ Blues for My Dog

⓯ Down the Road

Terrific! Wanna learn a faster rhythm? Turn the page...

YOU STILL GOT RHYTHM

Can you spare a quarter? How 'bout an eighth?

An **eighth note** has a flag on it:  or

Two eighth notes equal one quarter note or one beat. To make it easier on the eyes (you're welcome), eighth notes are connected with a **beam**:

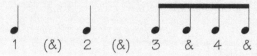
or

To count eighth notes, divide the beat into two and use "and" between the beats:

Practice this by first counting out loud while tapping your foot on the beat, then play the notes while counting and tapping:

What about the rest?

Eighth rests are the same, but you...pause. Count, tap, play, and pause with the following:

Now try playing a song that uses eighth notes. (Keep that foot going!)

18 Rockin' Riff

LESSON 6

You look sharp!

Remember when you were tuning (back on page 8), we used the terms "sharp" and "flat." Well, they're back, but slightly different.

Steppin' out...

Music is made up of **half steps** and **whole steps**. An easy illustration of this is seen on a piano keyboard. From one key to the next closest key is a half step; two keys apart is a whole step.

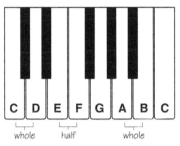

What about the notes in between?

Like the black keys on a piano, you also have some "in-between" notes on your saxophone. For example, notice that there is a note between F and G (one half step from each):

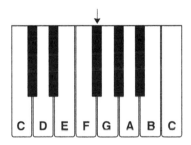

When a song requires a note that is only a half step higher or lower, a symbol is placed by that note.

One half step higher is called a **sharp** and looks like a tic-tac-toe board: ♯

One half step lower is called a **flat** and looks like a backwards note with no air in it: ♭

Exception to the rule...

From E to F is only a half step and from B to C is only a half step:

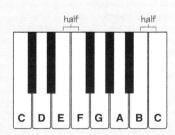

So, F is technically E-sharp and B is technically C-flat—but forget that. Turn the page and learn your first two "in-betweeners"...

Notes: B-flat, F-sharp

You're still in tune (hopefully), but the notes are intentionally "sharp" or "flat" here:

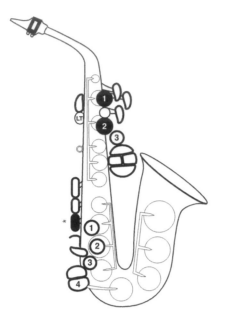

B-flat is on the same line as B but has the appropriate flat symbol next to it:

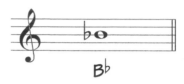

* This is a new key for you, located on the back of the sax.

 FINGERING MADE EASY: B-flat is one half step higher than A. Finger A and add the new key on the back of the sax. There are other fingerings for B-flat, too. Flip to page 46 and pick the one that you like best (for both comfort and sound).

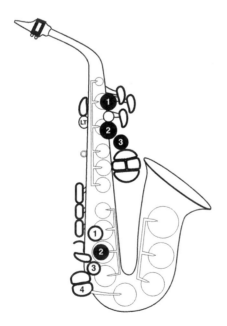

F-sharp occupies the same space as F but has the "tic-tac-toe" sharp sign:

 FINGERING MADE EASY: F-sharp is fingered with four keys just like F, but instead of RH finger 1 use RH finger 2 (one key lower).

Now let's try some tunes with your new "sharp-looking" (couldn't resist) notes...

IMPORTANT: When a sharp or flat appears in a measure, it applies through the entire measure. However, a **natural sign** (♮) cancels a sharp or flat, returning the note to its original "natural" pitch.

19 In the Concert Hall of the Mountain King

20 Aura Lee

21 Ode to Joyful Rock

☞ **Repeat signs** (|: :|) tell you to (you guessed it!) repeat everything in between. If only one sign appears at the end (:|), repeat from the beginning of the song.

Hey, look over here! Watch the music!
(Your brain has enough going on—don't try to memorize the tunes, too.)

LESSON 7
How low can you go?

Since the musical alphabet only has the letters A through G, repetition will eventually occur with all note names. Here's your first new note with a repetitive name...

Note: Low C

This will probably be your most difficult note (so far) to play. Hang in there and keep practicing:

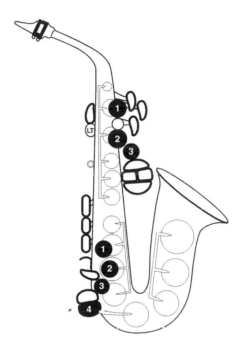

We're out of lines and spaces, so low C gets its own special **leger line**:

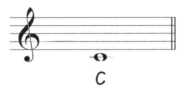

C

* make sure you press the lower key of these two keys.

 ADD A FINGER: Remember the (informal) rule—the lower the note, the more lower keys are pressed. As you play up from low C, remove lower keys.

Notice how the "add-a-finger" (or "lift-a-finger") approach works on this next exercise:

25 Add and Take

Now for two full pages of songs, using all ten different notes you've learned (but not all at once)...

◆ **26** Good Night, Fans

PRACTICE TIP: It may be helpful to finger through the song (without blowing) a couple of times before you play, so your fingers sort of learn where to go.

◆ **27** Yankee Doodle Rock

28 Swingin' the Old Chariot

29 Lazy Afternoon

30 Michael, Rock the Crowd Ashore

Instead of starting a song with rests (what a waste!), there's another solution...

Pickups aren't just trucks...

Instead of starting a song with rests, a **pickup measure** can be used. A pickup measure simply deletes the rests. So, if a pickup has only one beat, you count "1, 2, 3" and start playing on beat 4:

Try these songs with pickup measures:

31 When the Saints Go Marching In

32 Oh, Suzanna

Connect the dots...

Remember the dotted half note (three beats)? A **dotted quarter** note gets one and one-half beats:

quarter note   +   dot   =   dotted quarter note
(1 beat)   (1/2 beat)   (1 1/2 beats)

Think of it as being a quarter note tied to an eighth note.

Listen to tracks 33 and 34 while you clap the beat. Once you can feel the rhythm of the dotted quarter note, try playing it...

33 Worried Man Blues

34 I've Been Rocking on the Railroad

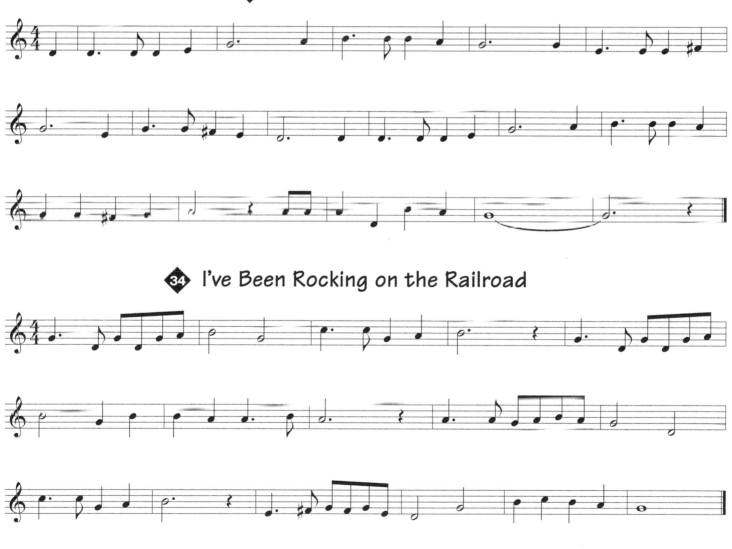

WARNING: If you haven't slept since page 1,
continuing could be hazardous to an enjoyable sax life.
Take a long break and go sleep!

LESSON 8
C to shining C...

Of the ten notes you've learned, the highest note (C) and lowest (low C) have the same name. But there's even more of a relationship between these two notes—they're one **octave** apart...

Octaves

An octave means eight notes apart. Notes with the same name are always an octave (or sometimes even two octaves) apart. If the word "octave" sounds familiar to you, it's because you have a key on your saxophone called the **octave key** (located just above your left thumb).

You'll be amazed by what you can do with it! With just one key, you can learn seven more notes in less than one minute. Don't believe us? Play the notes D through C along with track 35:

Now play them again (same fingering) with track 35, but this time hold down the octave key with your left thumb as you finger each note. You'll be playing these seven new notes:

Added bonus!

While we're bragging, the octave key also works with F-sharp and B-flat. (Okay, so you learned nine new notes in less than a minute. It's not called **FastTrack**™ for nothing!)

☞ EXCEPTION TO THE RULE: Low C and C are an octave apart but don't use the octave key approach. Remember to finger them separately.

Before playing some octaves in track 37, pencil in the names of your new high octave notes. (Leger lines can be confusing!)

37 Rocktaves

Writing in note names is a good idea for any music you play, especially songs that use high octaves. Don't be embarrassed to mark up your score—even the pros do it!

38 Pencil This!

Here's a well-known song that employs an octave "leap" right in the first measure (get your lead out and pencil away):

39 Take Me Onto the Stage Please

HELPFUL HINT: Try to let your eyes read ahead of the note that you're actually playing so that you're ready for the next set of notes.

40 Pack Up Your Troubles

And now, please rise and put those new notes to the test with an all-American favorite...

41 Star-Spangled Banner

Time for another break!
Call some friends and have them learn other **FastTrack**™ instruments,
so you can form a band.

LESSON 9

Something's fishy...

You know all the lines and spaces on the staff, as well as some leger lines on top and bottom. Let's play all the notes from low C to high C (traveling up two octaves!)...

42 ◆ C to C to C

Do you realize what you just played? That was your first musical scale—C Major. And a two-octave scale at that!

What's a scale?

Scales are arrangements of notes in specific patterns of half-steps and whole-steps. Most scales have eight notes with the top and bottom notes being an octave apart. The one you just played started on C and used a **major pattern**, thus it was the **C Major** scale.

Here are two more (single octave) scales...

43 ◆ G Major Scale

You aren't limited to just major scales. Try a **minor** one...

44 ◆ A Minor Scale

What's in a name?

As you can see (and hear), major scales are no larger or any more important than minor scales—it's just a name. Two things give a scale its name: the scale's lowest note (called the **root** note) and the **pattern** of whole steps and half steps used.

Pick a pattern...

Using piano diagrams to illustrate, the step pattern for a **major scale** is:

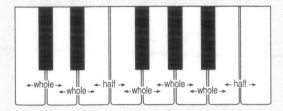

The step pattern for a **minor scale** is slightly different:

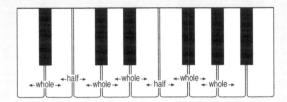

You can build major and minor scales beginning on any key simply by using these patterns and playing sharps and flats where appropriate.

Here are three more scales—one major and two minor:

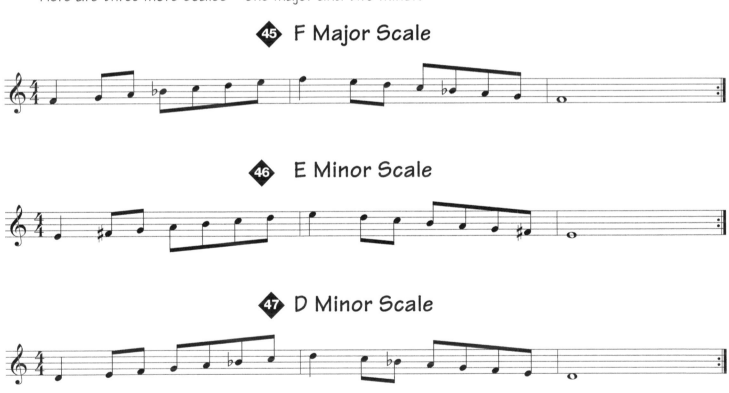

45 F Major Scale

46 E Minor Scale

47 D Minor Scale

Why bother?

 Playing scales helps build dexterity (nice word, huh?) in fingering notes.

 Songs and riffs are based on scales, so knowing the correct notes of a scale helps you to improvise a better solo.

Keys, please...

A song based on the C major scale is said to be in the **key of C**. Since the C Major scale has no sharps or flats, songs and riffs in the key of C also have no sharps or flats. Similarly, songs in the **key of F** will have one flat (just like the F Major scale).

48 Red River Rock

But rather than have a symbol by every flat (or sharp) in a song, a **key signature** can be used at the beginning of each line to indicate which notes are flat (or sharp) throughout the song.

Here's another song in the key of F. The key signature tells you to play all Bs as B-flat...

49 Rockin' on Old Smoky

key signature

Attention **FastTrack**™ shoppers!
Saxophone Songbook 1 is now available in music stores everywhere,
featuring hits by The Beatles, Clapton, Hendrix and many more.

Now for some songs in different keys—the first one in the key of G (notice the key signature):

◆50 Bach Rock

The next song looks like it has no key signature, but no sharps or flats generally means you're in the key of C:

◆51 Little Rock Band

Remember to practice slowly and speed up the tempo only after you feel confident with the notes and fingerings.

Major vs. minor

Songs can also be based on minor scales. Flip back to page 32 and notice that the F Major scale and D minor scale both have one flat. Thus, a key signature with one flat could mean the **key of F** or the **key of D minor**.

How can you tell? Just listen—major keys generally sound "happy;" minor keys generally sound "sad." Track 52 is in the key of E minor.

52 House of the Rising Sun

Sounds minor or "sad." Here's another (but in the key of A minor)…

53 Scarborough Fair

It's definitely time for another break.
Grab your remote and be a couch potato for a while—you deserve it!

LESSON 10

Feeling blue?

Before we learn to play the blues, we need to learn another note...

Note: E-flat

It's been a while since you learned new notes, so hopefully you haven't forgotten how a diagram works?!

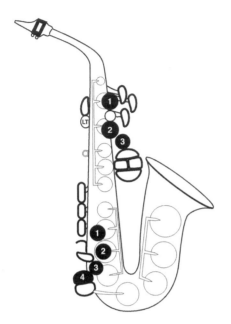

E-flat lies on the same line as E with the appropriate flat symbol next to it. Add the octave key for one octave higher:

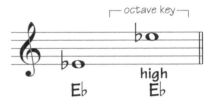

 FINGERING MADE EASY: E-flat is one **half step** higher than D. Finger D, then add half of the key under RH finger 4.

Try your new note in a blues scale starting on low C:

54 C Blues Scale

The **blues scale** (which you just played) is closely related to the minor scale, but it has two unique characteristics: it has only seven notes and employs a **one and a half step** (W+H):

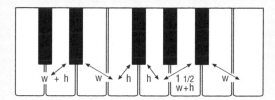

Try another blues scale—this time with A as the root note...

55 A Blues Scale

You can create some very cool blues riffs with this scale pattern (or with just parts of it).

☞ IMPORTANT: The next has a **1st** and **2nd ending** (indicated by brackets and the numbers "1" and "2"). Play the song once to the repeat sign (1st ending), then repeat from measure 1. The second time through, skip the 1st ending and play the 2nd (last) ending.

56 Faster Blues

Commit all of your scale patterns to memory—major, minor and blues!
Use them to create cool riffs, scales and solo melodies for other root notes.

LESSON 11
You got style!

How you play is as important (if not more important) as what you play. Here are some techniques to bring a little style into your music...

Glissando

A nice effect in sax music is a **glissando** (or "gliss"). It means to slide from one note to another, fingering (but not tonguing) the notes in between very quickly.

Glissandi (the plural form of this Italian word) are most commonly used between notes that are an octave apart. (But, hey, you can gliss between any two notes.) Listen to two examples on track 57:

Let's play a gliss from D to B. Play D and then release the lower keys quickly in order (while you continue to blow) until you get to LH finger 1 (B):

58 My Bonnie

Trill

Another cool technique is the **trill**, which means to alternate quickly between two notes that are close to each other (usually either a half step or whole step apart). Check out how this sounds on track 59:

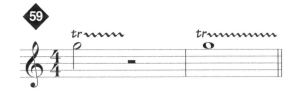

Start with G and trill between G and A by quickly releasing and pressing LH finger 3's key:

60 Just Trillin'

38

Slur

A curved line called a **slur** looks like a **tie**, except that it appears above (or below) two or more different notes (ties are used between same notes). A slur tells you to play the notes as smoothly as possible and only tongue the first note.

Listen to track 61 and notice which notes are tongued. Then you try it.

 PLAYING TIP: Continue to blow throughout a slurred phrase of music. Tongue the first note only and try not to breathe during a slurred phrase.

61 My Sunshine

Staccato

The opposite of a slur, **staccato** means to play short. This is marked by a dot above or below the notehead. To play staccato, tongue the note but only the "t" sound (not the entire "taaa"). Listen and then try it:

62 Staccato Funk

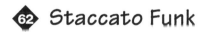

A songwriter will usually indicate these techniques in a song, but don't be afraid to improvise. Just mark appropriate places in the music for a gliss, trill, slur or staccato and let 'em rip!

EVERYTHING AND THE KITCHEN SYNC

In addition to playing techniques, there are rhythmic techniques that can really liven up an otherwise dull melody...

Syncopation

Syncopation is simply playing notes "off the beat." It makes the music sound less predictable (and, hey, it's great to dance to). Listen to a non-syncopated example:

63 Not Quite

With syncopation, you'll often encounter some new rhythms such as the **eighth-quarter-eighth** pattern and **tied eighths** pattern. Listen to track 64 as you count, then try clapping the rhythm.

With practice, you'll begin to recognize and play these patterns without even needing to count.

Now try the same song as track 63 above, but this time with syncopation:

65 Just Right

You can still feel the beat, but it certainly has a hipper groove to it.

Your turn!

Try playing these songs with syncopation. Stress the notes that have an accent mark ">" by the notehead (most of which will not be on the downbeat)…

66 You've Got a Saxophone in Your Hands

67 St. James Infirmary

Syncopation's as easy as that! Practice this page again—bet you can't keep from dancing.

GOOD THINGS TO KNOW

We're getting close to the end of the book (and the grand finale jam session). So, let's take a moment to learn a couple of important non-playing things about your saxophone.

Transposition

If you play with a band, you may notice that the music they're reading appears in a different key than yours. Don't panic—the music is right! The saxophone is a **transposing** instrument. Alto and baritone saxophones are based on the key of E-flat; tenor and soprano saxophones are based on the key of B-flat.

However, a piano, guitar and bass are all based on the key of C. This means that if you play a C on a piano and a C on a saxophone at the same time (hey, a one-man band), you'll hear two different notes. The alto saxophone will actually sound like the piano's E-flat note. (Why? Just suffice it to say that it's how the instruments are built.)

To compensate for this difference, music is "transposed" to the correct keys for each instrument so that all are playing the same **sounding** notes.

So, if an alto sax part is this...   the same part for piano would be this...

When you purchase music to play with a band, make sure the individual parts are transposed.

Clean as a whistle

Unless you got your sax for free (you lucky dog!), you've invested a bit of money. So, it's important to keep it in good condition, and that means to keep it clean and dry.

It's easy to clean your sax. You can buy a customized cleaning rag from instrument dealers, or you can make one yourself:

1 Tie one end of a string around the corner of a soft rag.

2 Tie the other end of the string to a small weight that won't scratch. (A magnet is good.)

3 Remove the neck and mouthpiece and place the weight into the bell of the body of the sax.

4 Turn the sax upside down until the weight falls out the neck-side of the body.

5 Pull the rag slowly through the body of the sax.

6 Repeat steps 3-5 several times and apply the same steps to the neck of the sax.

7 Wash the mouthpiece with warm water (no soap, please!) and dry it thoroughly.

8 Replace worn out reeds as often as necessary.

LESSON 12

Time to charge admission...

This isn't really a lesson...it's a jam session!

All of the FastTrack™ books (saxophone, guitar, keyboard, bass and drums) have the same last section. This way, you can either play by yourself along with the tracks or form a band with your friends.

So, whether the band's on the recording or in your garage, let the show begin...

68 **69** **Exit for Freedom**
minus sax   full band

70 **71** Unplugged Ballad

minus sax / full band

72 **73** Billy B. Badd

minus sax / full band

A **Intro**

Rock 'n' Roll

B **Verse**

C **Bridge**

D **Outro**

Bravo! Encore!!

Remember to practice often and always try to learn more about your instrument.

WAIT! DON'T GO YET!

Even though we hope (and expect) that you will review this entire book again and again, we thought you might like a "cheat sheet," referencing all the notes you've learned (and many you haven't learned until now). Well, Happy Birthday!

Fingerings

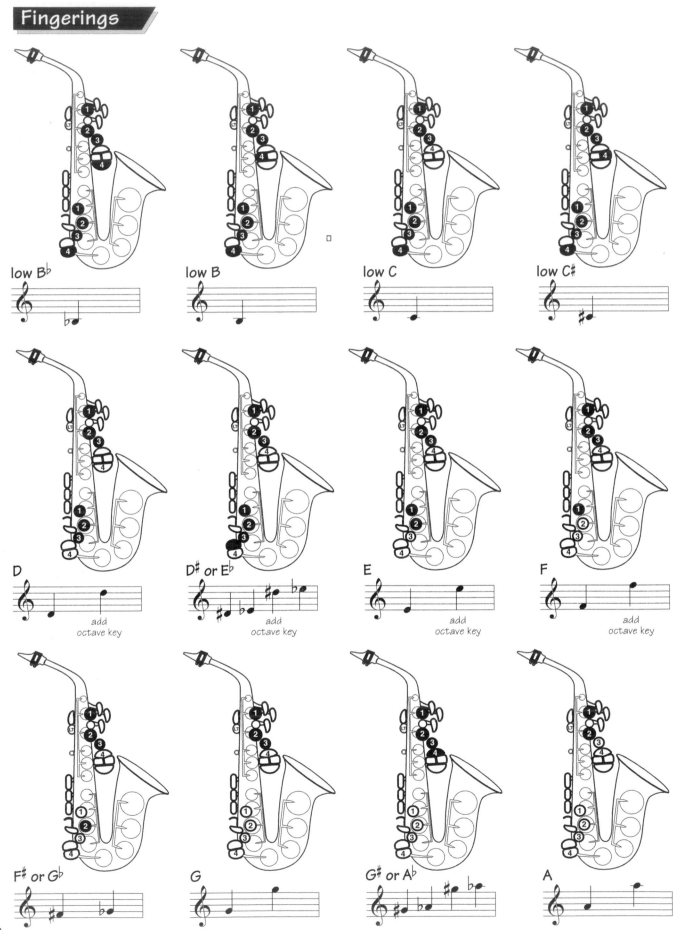

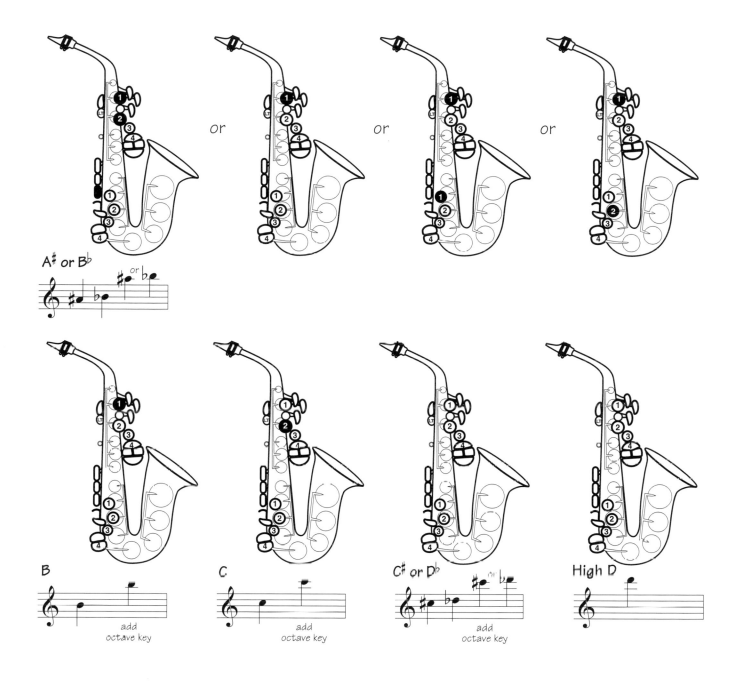

What now?

Here are some suggestions to help you continue to master the saxophone:

⭐1 **Repetition is the best way to learn.** Review the exercises in this book again and again until all the notes are easily playable without even thinking about the fingerings.

⭐2 **Buy FastTrack™ Saxophone Songbook**, which includes great songs from The Beatles, Clapton, Hendrix, and more!

⭐3 **Enjoy what you do.** Whether it's practicing, playing, jamming, or even cleaning your sax, do it with a smile on your face. Life's too short.

See you next time...

SONG INDEX

(...what book would be complete without one?)